Sunset Szn 2

Sunset SZN 2

Sunset Szn, Volume 2

Sakari Lacross

Published by Sakari Lacross, 2023.

SUNSET SZN 2

First edition. June 21, 2023.

ISBN: 979-8230477235

Written by Sakari Lacross.

Table of Contents

Side A

Perfect Sunset

Poem # 1

Nobody else at the beach
Just you and I
Years away from the sun
Orange ocean and sky
~ Pretend Sunsets

Poem # 2

I'm so used
To being by myself
So I push girls like you
Away.
You've been my type
I'm just...
Used to not being
Yours.
~ Cold Like Seattle

Poem # 3

You blush about him
Like he can do anything.
Anything means everything
In your mind.
He can be anything
To you, it means your everything.
I can't compete with that.
~ I Stare @ Sunsets Alone

Poem # 4

Chipped mirrors in our castle
She's still just now telling me things
My brokenness is on repeat
More poetry, that comes forth from you
~ I Need Your Closure

Poem # 5

Tempe palm trees
And Flagstaff leaves
I'm about to run off with his ex
To AZ
Tucson night lights
Avondale joy rides
I'm about to take his ex with me
To AZ
~ She Follows Me, To AZ

Poem # 6

Dimples in my lower back
She's always touching them.
V-line on my lower stomach
She runs her fingers down
And I'm sucking on her waistline
Because it's my first time tasting her
There's no reason for me to back out
It's my first time inside of her
~ We're Finally Past, Being Anxious

I Found Her Dreams

Poem # 7

I've been trying to eat her soul
From a distance
Distribution to her spirit
I'm being specific...when we sext.
I've been visualizing her next to me
Sunday through Wednesday
Because on Thursday
We're on Video chat.
Is it the worst thing to happen?
You fall in love, with my lustful sense
Of seeing things.
You're being yourself, and so am I.
~ Nothing To Our Lust

Poem # 8

Sex while you cook, take a break
And check the food
That's more exciting.
Something different, it makes a big difference
Because this time when I finish
I'll finish strong.
~ Something Oh So Different

Poem # 9

You dreamed about me before
You told me.
Reading my poetry, before you go to bed
Back against the headboard, where was my head?
I know where to fill in the blanks
I was climbing back up afterwards, wasn't I?
~ Ocean Licks

Poem # 10

I was wondering through a forest
Somewhere foreign
Did I belong anywhere
Before I ended up here
The sun said you were east
I was walking from the north
A brighter light, came from the west
When I find you baby, I'm going south
~ Looking For Your Sex

Poem # 11

An indirect kiss.
You kiss something, then I'll kiss
That same item.
We wouldn't be cheating.
~ You'll Still Be Faithful, To Your Man

Poem # 12

If I could get me some you
I'd have all my daily needs.
The vitamins I need.
That purpose...I need.
Maybe tomorrow will be different
If I had me some you.
A full drink of you.
Where would the time go?
~ A Dosage Of You

Poem # 13

Waters bouncing from you
And then landing on the floor
Sex in the shower.
Something complicated but achievable
A challenge by chance
Sex upside down.
And on the edge of the bed
We end up
Laying for a moment
Before...we stand up
~ Flowers For Yourself

Poem # 14

Like a paintbrush
You rub yourself on me
Something to endorse you
Before you direct me
I'm intrigued.
Coming down with me
Sinking from the couch
You whisper with me
On the living room floor
Whispers, in a librarian's tone
~ Our Own Erotica

Poem # 15

I'm over-fantasizing
We're on a roof.
And on this roof, there's no sunlight
You're there too.
On this roof, you're naked
I'm naked too.
And on this roof, there's no one for miles
So we can do...
~ The Unthinkable

Poem # 16

She's moaning, tired, helpless
And controlling.
She's inspired, interested, thoughtful
And creamy.
But I eat it, put it in, take it out
And eat it again.
I finger, suck on her, and catch her waters
As they come out.
~ Stay/Lay

Colored Leaves

Poem # 17

My new crush, I heart all of your pics
I'd take the M from your name, if you were offering it
By this time, I'm not busy enough
To lose updates, on you
~ My New Crush

Poem # 18

I see another mistake
Added to me
~ Self Conscious Efforts

Poem # 19

Nowadays
I remind myself
To think less with my emotions
And to dwell more
On my experiences
~ Finding Something, To Overshadow My Negativity

Poem # 20

Written in the earth's dirt, was her name
I believe, she once touched this ground.
The people she's around, don't know
They're around, someone special.
~ Someone Oh So Special

Poem # 21

Trying to beat the odds
My own heart, is against me.
Because even when I'm available
I'm only available...for her
~ This Heart Is Her's, In My Chest

Poem # 22

My heart has mood stripes
Different colors, during the cold of the year
And I feel like
I didn't give you, my brightest of colors
~ I Understand Where Things Went Wrong

Poem # 23

You're looking
The opposite way of me
And I'm looking
At the back of your head
Wondering with my headphones on
What type of mini world, takes your interest
~ What Does Your World Look Like?

Poem # 24

Gleaming touch
She only knows light
On her surface
So my shadows shrift
Though yesterday
My shadows, almost reached you
~ Most Likely You Don't Realize, How Important U R 2 Me

Poem # 25

She's a cherry blossom tree
I stand by, catching all of her
Fallen leaves
Her petals touch my hands
And heal
~ She's Pink Grace

Poem # 26

I used to always
Want open doors
Closed.
Wanting answers, to "what if"
Now I leave those doors open
Staring down
Empty hallways
~ Empty Hallways

The Last Sunset

Poem # 27

At this point, fear has stopped me
Whoever gets your heart, just gets it
Sakari

Poem # 28

I let my mother back in
Her loyalty, still being with my father
Don't hold it against me.
I went for a woman who fed me emptiness
She chose another me, and went against me
Don't hold it against me.
I caught feelings for a girl that's walking distance, from where I stay
I broke my own rules, she knows where I lay
Don't hold it against me.
I've missed my therapy sessions, and I feel like
Imma break soon
Don't hold it against me.
Life's no good for me
I just wanna fuck Jazz before I die
I want three girls in mind
None of which, at the same time.
Can't give into my demonic side
I don't feel like an angel inside
If my father dies, it's from the pills killing him
Inside.
I'm dark hearted in a void
It's hard for me to not smile back, at a pretty girl

Don't hold it against me.
I've got three phones, but I only call you
On one
Don't hold it against me.
When you held me the last time
I cried to you, about my childhood
Don't hold it against me.
We're not together, but we're still having sex
You've been pregnant twice by me, but both my kids died
I don't hold it against you.
Life's no good for me
I just wanna fuck Jazz before I die
I want three girls in mind
None of which, at the same time.
Can't give into my demonic side
I don't feel like an angel inside
If my father dies, it's from the pills killing him
Inside.
~ Things Off The Record(Can't Hold It Against Me)

Poem # 29

We're not shining, in the apocalypse
Everything is so much more, hardcore
Than you and I, can comprehend
Temporarily, undermined
~ The World Ending, With You & I...

Poem # 30

His craft revolves around your likes
So he may be, your light.
You no longer relish, in my art
My moments, represent your dark.
~ I Stopped Trying To Win Hearts

Poem # 31

We're doing the least
In my mind
My imagination
Can't even lie
~ Who Really Wins You

Poem # 32

There's never enough you, to go around
I'm always the one, left out
~ Waiting Outside Of Your Job

Poem # 33

Seeing stars with you
Waking up during sunsets with you
~ My Planned Later Days

Poem # 34

But I don't see, those other people.
Those guys in your background, don't bother me.
I'd never let you know otherwise
Because I wouldn't want to stress you
With my insecurities
~ You Deserve, Someone Brave

Poem # 35

In a world full of losers
I need to know, I have nothing to worry about.
That no matter who places a smile on your face
You'd only frown...over me.
That infatuation slips your mind
And that you pay those nameless fiends...no mind.
~ Only Mine

Poem # 36

Life's too short
For me to always spend it
Being mad.
Being ungrateful
I'd rather stick with my sadness.
I don't wanna be, the hateful guy...
~ Don't Wanna Hate This World, Anymore

Time Away From The Internet

Poem # 37

I'm falling down the mountain
You had me climb.
No rope to hang from
You told me on the way down
That my world Without you
Would be just fine.
How do you know that?
I've never lived with or without you...
~ Do You Actually Believe, You'd Serve No Purpose, In My World

Poem # 38

All the flowers you had me smell
Were poisonous
~ My Poison Ivy

Poem # 39

The emptiest of carts.
Being in your grocery store
Your customers never seem
To fill me with anything.
~ Dead On Arrival Emotions, You Bring Me No Joy

Poem # 40

Who else feels empty
After putting their phone down?
Back on the internet, I shouldn't go
Picking back up, where I left off.
~ I'm Searching For Something, I Just Don't Know What

Poem # 41

You can't let go of two
You can't let go.
I remember sixteen conversations later
You told me, I was never pathetic
~ You Could Never Give Me A Reason, Why I Couldn't Have You

Poem # 42

Too depressing
I don't want to reach underneath your skin
In that way
So I'll wait for Summer to come.
I'll wait for the township skies
To match your glow
Because I'm always so gloomy
So there's no way
I can enhance your glow.
Chased down by my own
Alienated emotions
I'd be crazy enough to wear my hoodie
During the summer seasons
Walking past, with you in the corner of my eye.
~ I Shouldn't Be Able To Dream About You, For Free

Poem # 43

I'm sorry
But I wish we could go to the moon together
Or at least...
Be warm together, underneath, the night's stars.
I don't sleep much
It isn't good for me.
I don't hang out much
It isn't good for me.
I know...
That you'll be good for me.
~ You'd Be Underneath The Night's Sky With Me, On Fresh Cut Grass

Poem # 44

I'm hoping for intimacy
Where anything feels possible.
Possibly becoming parts of you
Making us a cyborg, in a dystopia
~ The Year 2122

Poem # 45

This whole time, I'm wondering...
"How do I make this more,"
Seeing your lonely hands
Direct themselves
~ I'm Walking Behind You, When You Need Me

Poem # 46

And I've been trying to find a reason
To come back to the coffee shop.
Trying to find a reason
Without breaking myself.
But if you'd meet me in the parking lot...
Same time, everyday...
I'll be there.
Same time, every day...
~ The Wind's On Your Side

Orange Skies

Poem # 47

I can't be wrong
For wanting to exist
Around you
~ I Want To Co-Exist

Poem # 48

I'm holding on to invisibles
I imagine by glance, how you'd feel.
I wish you could feel my depression
These poems...don't scratch the surface
~ Underneath The Invisible Surface

Poem # 49

For the first time
I prayed to see a girl
To later meet this girl
Where the darkness inside of me
Couldn't reach...
~ The Girl Who I Believed, To Correct Me

Poem # 50

Save me for better things
I'm more human than you think.
All I can think about
Are static visions, in the sky
Static skies
Don't know where I'm going
When I finally die
Static skies
~ Static Skies

Poem # 51

I'm no longer mad
At the guys who are trying.
I'm mad at the guys
You're giving opportunities to
~ You Rarely Choose/I Can't Mature, With So Little Exp.

Poem # 52

Body motionless
Your eyes no longer blink.
You realize that your soul has been sealed away
In a body...that you want out of
~ Somewhere, We're All Self Conscious

Poem # 53

More and more stars
Are disappearing
Does it feel to you
That morning has arrived, too soon?
~ A Starless Sky

Poem # 54

With magic itself
With honey unblended
With love of some shape
With hearts that are see-through
You scatter yourself, before the day's end.
With promises in the sky
And feet on the clouds
With hugs that feel like air
Your visuals, pass through me
You scatter yourself, before the day's end.
~ Scattered You

Poem # 55

Where does the motivation go
When you're not going anywhere
Where does it go?
When everything you would spend time on
Becomes neglected
Where is your motivation, when hope becomes less
~ Agree With Me, I'm A Loser, Right?

Those Other Nights

Poem # 56

I know me.
If I come around more often
I'll eventually want you, climbing on me.
You stopped me outside of your job.
Mentioned that you haven't seen me in a while
I've stayed out the way.
Trying my best not to make eye contact
But your eyes of Santorini...
And your smile that locks up your tongue...
My mind wonders, underneath the surface.
That surface on your figure
That you call skin
Your voice sounds like
Butterfly wings.
And I didn't try to, but I kept making you laugh.
And you didn't try to, but you kept making me smile.
I wouldn't mind
Getting in trouble with you
~ You Still Slow Dance, In My Mind

Poem # 57

I'm begging for more
Those chills and addictions
You have left me with
I'm begging for more...
~ Those Other Nights Interlude

Poem # 58

Under my blankets, I'm searching for you
A year prior, from how things came off
You've become an EP
To my collection of memories
~ I Still Feel Her

Poem # 59

Nothing about me
Is all that stand out.
I'll get a coffee, and ask for you
At the front counter.
You'll appear busy, but never leave me
Hanging
~ I Appreciate Your Voice

Poem # 60

Not giving you sweet me
I'm giving you, honest me.
Not giving you moments
I'm giving you, timelines.
Not giving...
Not giving...
Not going too vulnerable, unless you have the time
I'm not giving years of see through walls
Not asking for her attraction of any sorts
I'm not giving lust to another body
Not giving...
Not giving...
~ Not Giving Myself, Permission To Be Accepted

Poem # 61

I can imagine you
Once again
Sucking all the fluids out of me
Leaving me drained.
Forcing everything out of me
Unexpected, head rest.
~ Your Head, Resting On My Stomach, Afterward

Poem # 62

Doing it the honest way
You tell me to pilot
And be myself
You give me a time limit
An entire night
To envelop you
~ Time Gated

Poem # 63

Place me on your moon
The fullest part of you
How do I fulfill you
In only a night
~ Making The Other Half Of Your Moon

Poem # 64

Things are changing
You're my underground fan
This time
Tonight...
I'm misunderstood
And seeking guidance
~ Her Taste Has Changed

Poem # 65

I keep the pillow you screamed in
The last time you were over
The closest to me
~ Her Pleasure Pillow

Poem # 66

Your body's now...
On its last song
An outro's to be expected.
You're gaining those same chills
I get right before...
I can't explain
~ We Can't Say The Last Time

Poem # 67

Blowing into your open window
You expected, more from my wind
But I don't have much of a breeze within me
You take too much of my air
Deep breaths in between
You leave me with just enough oxygen, to rest a bit
~ The Only Girl, To Make Me Tap Out

Shoreline

Poem # 68

I tell you how I feel
And you leave me on seen
I tell you how I feel
And you leave me alone
What did I say wrong?
Compliments to your skin
What did I say wrong?
I told you the truth
I knew I wasn't worthy
Worthless by myself
You probably know
You're more than my worth
~ Back Under A Rock, I Go

Poem # 69

I'm thinking, but I'm not crying
In the shower, but I'm not showering
Water running loud enough
You'll never hear, how I feel again
~ Showers Don't Tell

Poem # 70

You're not mines, why would you stay?
You're not mines, why wouldn't you leave?
Offer me to come inside, I could only dream
~ Someplace Better, Than Here With Me/Maybe A Dream Come True

Poem # 71

You don't treat a woman wrong
Because she doesn't want you
You just hide away, hopefully becoming
Something she does want
~ Maybe In The Future

Poem # 72

I'll be here when you're done
Getting your heartbroken
From all those other guys
~ I'm Not Rushing Your Heart

Poem # 73

At least you see my messages
You don't have to reply.
You see my messages
At least you know, I'm here.
~ You Acknowledge I Exist

Poem # 74

Tell me to come get lost
Where did your waves go?
Ocean breeze, with October winds
It's unfair to me, but I'll swim
In your cold waters
~ Lost At Your Sea

Poem # 75

5pm, almost looks like you
Orange Tucson skies
A sight by the edge
Of an open freeway
5pm takes inspiration
Giving credit to its owner
You could sue the skies
If mentioned otherwise
~ You Look Like 5pm, In Arizona

Poem # 76

That's all I want.
Make me believe
That I've got a chance.
Even if I don't have a chance
Mislead me.
~ My Greatest Art, Comes From Misdirection

Poem # 77

With long hair on an island
You stare off into the sea.
A slimmer of clouds await
Though no other storm
Would look as captivating
As the one
On this island
~ Another Story

Autumn Wind

Poem # 78

Soul touching
You hugged my spirit
And then left me feeling
Less than physical
~ Less Than Feeling

Poem # 79

You've got the ability
To answer all my questions
About myself
~ I Imagine Feelings Of Comfort, From Hugging You

Poem # 80

You don't want me in that way
Just be my friend.
Don't ignore me
I'll settle...for being friends
~ Be My Friend Please

Poem # 81

Feels like I've slowed down my heartbeat
So I won't feel, so easily
If my heart stopped, anytime soon
Would you ever care to say, that you knew me
~ I Wanted You To Get To Know Me

Poem # 82

I know that guy
That you message in the mornings
Asking if he's ok
Stays blessed
~ You Bring On Him Infinite Blessings

Poem # 83

Instead of falling in love
I could have been honing
My art.
~ Seeking Another, Set Me Back

Poem # 84

Her pretty
Is already
Being given
Natural relations
~ Natural Touches

Poem # 85

Yesterday, I backed away
Today, you want me in close
Poetry that leaves paper
You leave me, in the Autumn Wind
~ Autumn Wind

Poem # 86

You're warmer than you were
Yesterday
Is today
Better for you yet?
~ I Care To Myself, Staring Your Way

Poem # 87

There will be days
He hurts your feelings
And I'll be there
~ Winds Blow In Both Directions

See You In The Next Life

Poem # 88

I don't want a normal beauty
I want your celebrity body
Your breezing appearance.
2k book downloads, I now average a month
Without promo...
Without help...
I'm climbing Olympus, to meet you.
And you don't even know it.
You don't even know me.
But I dream...so often.
~ Another Dream To Me

Side B

Manifested Darkness

Poem # 89

I can't get to you, like I want to
Because of the law.
The law protects sheep
Like you.
Men who disrespect women
But fear other men.
I dream of being in a cage with you
You being...my chew toy
~ I'm A Dog To These Boneheads

Poem # 90

4 people deep
We stomp him out.
4 people deep
We swipe his soul.
4 people deep
We run in different directions.
4 people deep
We can't get caught, with these weapons...
~ No Mercy For A Nobody

Poem # 91

Biggie hit him
And knocked his dreads loose.
Devon slammed him
And he screamed.
My knee on his neck
He apologized.
Me and my brothers solve shit...
With violence.
~ How I Taught My Brothers

Poem # 92

The past lingers to me
Chains that rust, but refuse to break.
These chains of hatred...they are sever proof
Nowadays, it feels like I'm always angry.
The number one spot, in the hearts of others
Is mine!
The success from throwing myself, into my career
Is mine!
The way I hate the people in this world
Is mine!
~ My Hatred Of My Past, Pushes Me

Poem # 93

The Last time I spoke to my mother
She told me I had to let go of my hatred
Towards my father.
But I don't have to let go of anything.
I've let her go, once again.
She's siding with him, as always.
My mother used to tell me
That we were moving from state to state
To start a new life
Escaping my dad.
But you never gave me that new life, did you mom?
~ Source Of My Hatred

Poem # 94

Brown Oceans in a bottle
I often need this, to talk to you.
Those after work conversations, on the phone
I always bring up, the times you hurt me
Why did you hurt me?
So many times, I asked you not to
Does sorry mean, you're sorry for only that particular time?
I talk up our mess, and I wanna get past it
But why do these things, hurt so bad?
Why did you hurt me?
~ You Never Planned On Hurting Me, Is What They All Say

Poem # 95

You were the only thing, I wanted to learn.
Lingerie and Make Pretends
I wanted a 4.0, the semester I had you.
And I'm still in my twenties
So I know I've got some growing to do.
I'm still being taught things
Life being the principle, and these broken women
Being my Guidance Counselor
~ I Continue To Learn, Through Lust

At The Bottom, Somewhere

Poem # 96

When I come back to Arizona
You'll be at peace.
So much noise in your background
You can't rest.
I'm ready for you to die too, Pops.
~ The Only Thing We Agree On

Poem # 97

I'm sticking things out
But do I really need you?
I feel so upset right now
Angry, at the wrong people.
~ I Feel Robbed Of My Glory

Poem # 98

I'm lashing out
With a chain in my hand
I know you won't
Come home with me
~ My Inner Rebel

Poem # 99

If I get violent, would I still be
In your favor?
See my arms, covered in their blood
Would you hide me
When the sirens came?
~ Should I Move Forward, With My Knives In Hand

Poem # 100

He compliments your smile
He makes it his business...to ask about us.
He's a nobody. An abomination.
You tell me...there's nothing special about him.
I just sent you to work, with my water in you
He works with you, knowing...I'm fucking you.
Compliments he gives, but I don't need to.
Don't get that boy took off, and sent into the clouds
~ I Know You're Into Young Guys, Like Me (Not Guys Double My Age, Like Him)

Poem # 101

When I see him, I'm punching his face off
They can put me back in the cage.
Cement walls, I'm through caring
I don't give a fuck...about throwing my life away
~ My Response Is More Important

Poem # 102

Pick his stale body up
Off the ground, they carry him
The world didn't need him, anyway
Just another loser, cheating on his girl
At home.
~ This Time, He Pursued The Wrong Woman

Poem # 103

I may be difficult
But I've got feelings too
I show it by violence
I only want him hurt
Because he's so drawn to you
~ Add Him To My "2 Get" List

Poem # 104

If the police catch me, it's over
His body hit the ground, then rolled over
Wake up from my dream, my nightmares of going to Hell
Are over
~ I Dream About Malice

Poem # 105

On the Westside of Heaven
I'd like to believe
God will overlook
My mental health
And leave me...
I'm not a bad person
I'd like to believe
God will forgive my violent ways
I'd hope to see
~ On the Westside of Heaven, God will let me reside

Poem # 106

She's playing quarterback
With my glass essence
With no defense in front of her
She's throwing me, to whoever catches me
~ She Can't Help But Shatter Me

Poem # 107

With my heart
I take painkillers
With my heart
I'm being mistreated.
With my heart
She's mistaking me
With my heart
She's giving out pieces
With my heart
I'm feeling fatigue
With my heart
I'm catching my own tears
With my heart
I've been writing
With my heart
I'm being mistreated
~ With My Heart Interlude

Poem # 108

I paid attention
To how you never loved me
~ I Never Lost Focus

Poem # 109

Let's just be nothing to each other
You're already making new friends, anyway
I'll be the last ant on the hill
You've already made your way inside, with another batch
~ A Lonely Ant

Malice

Poem # 110

Bullets tear through his rib cage
That's what I asked for.
His body goes into shock
Mini tremors against the cold street
That's what I asked for.
~ Dark Wishes

Poem # 111

Half these men in this world
Don't deserve life
This world...is broken.
Erasing a few, like I drew them
There's only one God, for a reason
Because I would drown half this world
In the darkest of waters
I'd decide...who the fuck I wanted alive
~ Malice Interlude

Poem # 112

This patience, I don't have
I'm not from this side
In my dreams, corpses roll down
From the hillside.
His insides bleed out
That's how I got to know him
He existed in someone's timeline
Just not mine
These souls in life, aren't even worth keeping
~ Life Has A Way...Of Testing You

Poem # 113

I put it down
But now...it's time I picked it back up
My knife.
My blade
Tearing into souls
Skin so unprotected.
~ Killer Nature

Poem # 114

Suffocate him
Six feet below the earth
Rest away
You won't be missed by anyone, important
~ Buried Alive

Poem # 115

Skull knight
My devoted disciple.
My imaginary friend.
Wear their skeletons like armor
~ A Tortured Soul

Poem # 116

Bullet makes it through his neck
His head falls on his shoulder.
He used to complain about insomnia
He finally, gets to rest
~ Fuck Him (He Should've Been Dead)

Poem # 117

He dove into the black ocean
Black sharks, he wouldn't see
And in this water
Decomposing corpses
Never surface...
~ Black Oceans

Poem # 118

Proceed with caution
I don't like you much.
The rest of your existence
I see no need for
You're a fly, without its wings
~ I Refuse Your Welcoming

Poem # 119

I'm screaming into your decay
I hate you so much, is what they believe
But I never really hated you
I just got tired of waiting
For your undead natures, to change
~Your Decay

Don't miss out!

Visit the website below and you can sign up to receive emails whenever Sakari Lacross publishes a new book. There's no charge and no obligation.

https://books2read.com/r/B-A-GXQL-PHSKC

BOOKS 2 READ

Connecting independent readers to independent writers.

Did you love *Sunset SZN 2*? Then you should read *Never Ending*[1] by Sakari Lacross!

[2]

Over 90 poems of loneliness, unrequited feelings, lust and strong desires.

*I'm not worth the commitmentMy Heart's collapsed, and I don't believeThere's anyway to fix itYou'll be doing all the work, with the two of us.My spirits stay low, most of the dayYou'd be single, being my girlFeeling so distant, right next to meYou should leave, before you like me. *Single In A Relationship ~ Sakari**

1. https://books2read.com/u/4AAvpe

2. https://books2read.com/u/4AAvpe

Also by Sakari Lacross

A Dawn Breaking Romance

Romance Dawn

Beyond Dawn

A Final World

Rising Tides

Don't End Up Consumed

Don't End Up Consumed 2

Belonging

I Hope I Belong

I Hope I Belong Too

Eclipse

Eclipse: Side A

Eclipse Side B

Endless Journal

Epilogue

Eternal Flames

expression

My Soul Mate

The Only Girl I Really Want

Perfect Gentleman

Perfect Gentleman

Simp Undying

I Simp For You

I Simp For You Too

Another Reason To Simp

Soft Hardcover

New Love Plus(+)

Sunset Szn

Sunset Szn

Sunset SZN 2

Sunset SZN 3

The Last Witch

The Last Witch: Book 1
The Last Witch: Book 2

This Is For Her
Someone Like You
Someone Like You Too
Someone Else Like You

Threads
Threads

Standalone
The Legend Of Krampus
Deeper Than Magic
A Place Inside My Castle
Luminary
Loyalist To The Moon
Thoughts & Memories
Ideas & Reality
Vines & Beauty
V For Her
Playing With Skeletons

About the Author

Sakari Lacross was born February 5th, 1994, in Cleveland Ohio. Spending most of his childhood being raised in Flint Michigan, Sakari's mother moved him and his family to Arizona when he was 15. Sakari has been writing since he was nine years old, competing in his school's poetry contest and bimonthly writing events. Discovering all his true potential to write during his years he went to linden charter academy, Sakari won his first local poetry contest at Sam Garcia Western Avenue Library, located in Avondale Arizona. Sakari then published his first poetry collection, titled, PTSD.

www.ingramcontent.com/pod-product-compliance
Lightning Source LLC
La Vergne TN
LVHW091051150826
845673LV00002B/536

* 9 7 9 8 2 3 0 4 7 7 2 3 5 *